What a mess!

Let's help pick them up.

Draw a —— to show the ones that match.

Try it!

Next time a load of wash is done, help sort the socks into pairs. Someone will thank you!

Why did Wags wear orange socks?
Because his purple ones were in the wash!

Look! A path!

Follow the ◯s.

Color them ▬.

Where do they lead?

START HERE TO SEE THE VEGETABLES!

THIS WAY TO THE PUMPKINS!

VEGETABLES AHEAD!

VEGETABLES

—Try it!—

Find three pens or pencils. Use them to form a triangle. Then use one of the pens or pencils to draw triangles on a sheet of paper.

Math Skills: Identifying Geometric Shapes

Giant vegetables!

Which ones are biggest?

Draw a — from each to the biggest one.

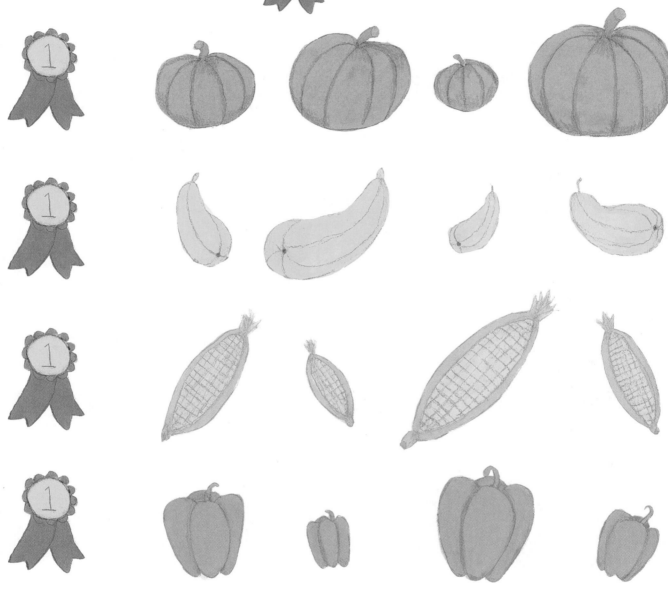

—Try it!—

Make a chart by taping together sheets of paper.
Tape the chart on a wall or back of a door. Measure
and mark the height of everyone in your family. Who
is the tallest person? Who is the shortest? Measure
again in six months. How much have you grown?

Basic Skills: Comparing Sizes **17**

Put them in order

Look at each row.
What happened first? Write 1.
What happened next? Write 2.
What happened last? Write 3.

—Try it!—

Collect some seeds from fruits and vegetables. Compare the seeds. Draw them. Why do you think plants have seeds?

Boo!
Knock, knock.
Who's there?
Jack.
Jack who?
Jack O'Lantern!

Win a giant pumpkin

Write your name on the ticket.
Have someone help you write your
address and telephone number.

YOU CAN WIN!
Write your name, address, and phone number.
Drawing October 1.

Name _____

Address _____

Phone Number _____

Everybody has more than one name. What is your
first name? Your last name? Do you have a middle
name or a nickname, too? What is it? Ask an adult
to write all your names in capital letters. Trace
over the letters with a crayon or marker.

Sweets to eat

What letter begins each one?

◯ the capital and lowercase letters.

 Aa | A   C   a

 Bb | b   B   A

 Cc | a   c   C

 Dd | D   d   C

—Try it! —

Study some supermarket ads. Look for pictures of food. Look at the letters and words, too. Find words that have these letters: **a, b, c,** and **d.** Circle those words. Ask someone to read the words to you.

Say this tongue twister fast:
   Buy a big, blue bucket of blue blueberries.
Now say it again three times, even faster.

Language Arts: Alphabet and Beginning Sounds

Your favorite fruit

The students are having a fruit party.
What did they bring? Answer the questions.

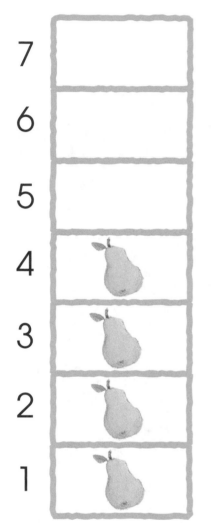

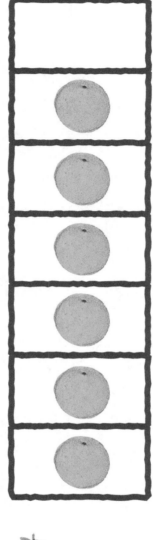

Try it!

Ask your family and friends
what fruit they like best.
Make a graph to show the
fruit most people like.

How many s?   3   6   2   4

How many s?   7   4   3   5

How many s?   6   3   5   7

How many s?   4   6   2   5

Math: Picture Graphs   21

It's a pioneer village

Everyone here does what people did long ago.

Well, almost everyone...

✗ things that don't belong in this long-ago scene.

—Try it! —

Look around your house. What do you see that would not have been in a house long ago? Would people have used something else instead? What would they have used?

What did you see?

Here are some things you saw in Pioneer Village.
What letter begins each one?
◯ the capital and lowercase letters.

Ee	E	e	C
Ff	d	f	F
Gg	G	b	g
Hh	b	H	h

What side of a goose has the most feathers?

The outside!

HA HA HA

—Try it!—

Divide a sheet of paper into four boxes. Write **Ee** in one section,
Ff in another, and **Gg** and **Hh** in the others. In each section,
draw a picture of something that begins with that letter.

Counting at Pioneer Village

Draw the next one in each row.

—Try it! —

Count the pictures again. This time count by twos:
2, 4, 6, 8. Try counting your toy cars, your books, even
your french fries by twos.

How many in all?
Write the number in each box.

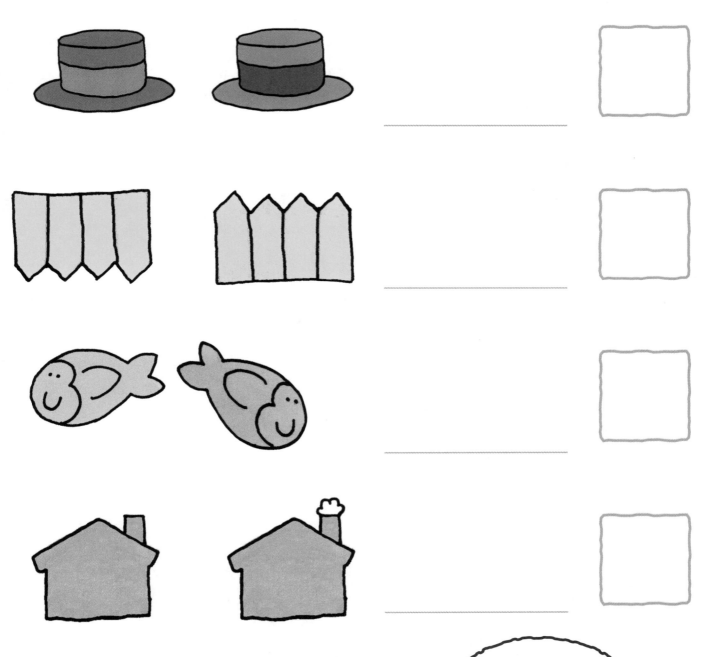

Two, four, six, eight,
Who do we appreciate?
Wags, Wags,
Hooray! Hooray!

Let's ride!

Hooray! Each of us has a ticket for three rides.

✓ your favorite ride.

Then count the kids. How many in all?_____

—Try it!—

Have you ever been on a ride? What was it like? Draw
a picture of the ride and tell someone about it.

Math: Counting   ©1999 School Zone Publishing Company

Fun and scary

What do you think of these rides?

◯ fun or scary—or both fun and scary.

fun   scary

fun   scary

fun   scary

fun   scary

—Try it! —

Divide a paper into four boxes. Draw a picture in each box. Draw
something that makes you happy, something that makes you sad,
something that makes you scared, and something that makes you mad.

     Science: Emotions   27

Opposites

Sometimes you're up, and sometimes you're down.
Draw ——s to match the opposites.

down

off

top

up

empty

full

on

bottom

—Try it!—

Stand in front of a full-length mirror. Stretch to make yourself tall.
Then squat to make yourself short. Can you make yourself happy
and sad? Can you make a scary face and a friendly face? What
other opposites can you do in the mirror?

More or less

Count the people on these rides.
Draw a —— under the set that has more people.

Who's bigger, Mr. Bigger or Mr. Bigger's baby?
Mr. Bigger's baby. She's a little bigger!

Who's hungry?

It's time for lunch!
Draw a —— from each food to its box.

—Try it!—

Think of some other foods. Draw pictures of them, cut them out, and place them on the box where they belong.

What's white on the outside, green on the inside, and hops?

A frog sandwich!

What's good to eat?

Plan a well-balanced meal.
Pick one food from each food group.
Draw it on the plate.

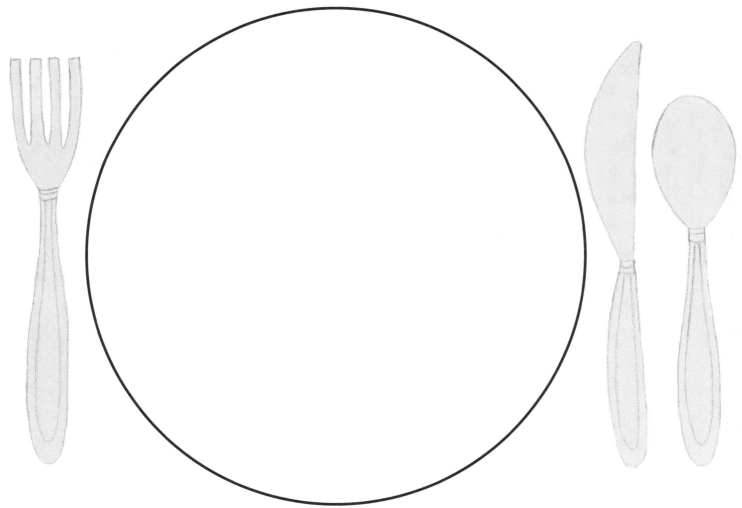

Try it!

Set the table for a meal. Remember to put the forks at the left of the plates and the knives and spoons at the right, just the way you see them here.

What are two things you can never have for breakfast?
Lunch and dinner!

Food—and a visitor

Here are some picnic foods and one visitor.

What letter does each one begin with?

◯ the capital and lowercase letters.

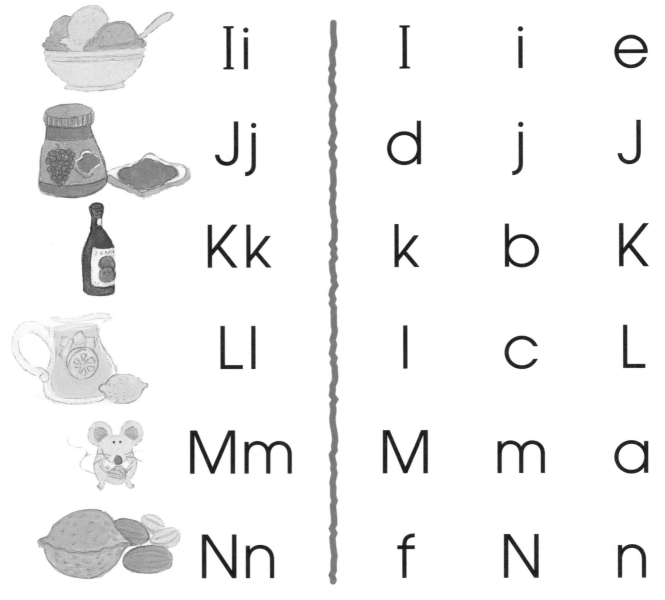

Ii	I	i	e
Jj	d	j	J
Kk	k	b	K
Ll	l	c	L
Mm	M	m	a
Nn	f	N	n

—Try it!—

Use chalk to draw a hopscotch game on a driveway or sidewalk. In each box, write one of these letters. When you toss your marker in, name the letter in the square in which it lands.

Knock, knock.
Who's there?
Lettuce.
Lettuce who?
Let us in, we're hungry!

Cleanup time

Draw ——s to put the items in the correct recycle bins.

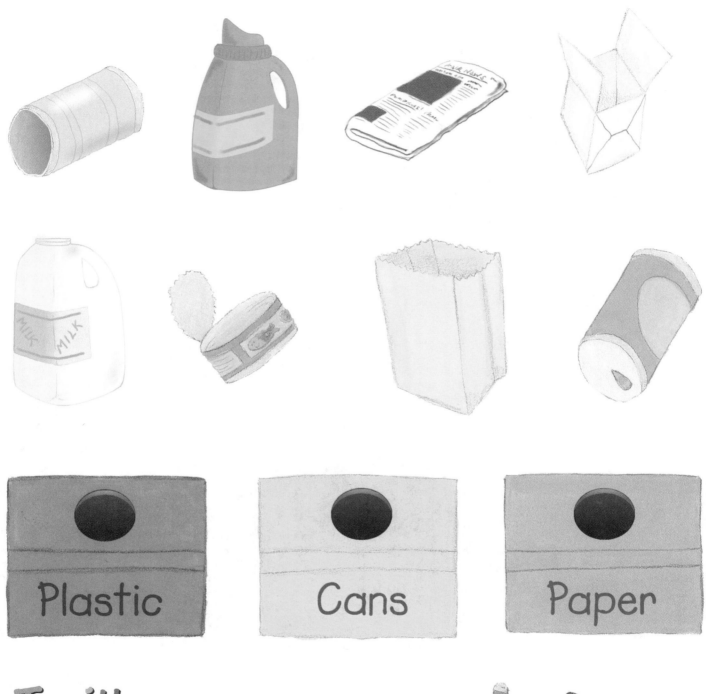

—Try it!—

Here's a way to recycle soft-drink cans. Wash them out and use them as blocks. You can stack them to make towers or line them up to build walls. What else can you do with the cans?

Science: Recycling 33

At the gift shop

How much do the gifts cost?
Draw a —— from the coins to the gifts.

STICKERS 5¢

TOY ANIMALS 10¢

PENNY CANDY 1¢

POSTCARDS 25¢

1¢   5¢   10¢   25¢

—Try it!—

What would you like to buy at the gift shop? Collect some pennies. Count the number of pennies you need to buy the item you want. Then pick a gift for a friend and count the pennies you need to buy it.

Shop for the alphabet

Lots of fun things are for sale in the gift shop.

What letter begins each one?

◯ the capital and lowercase letters.

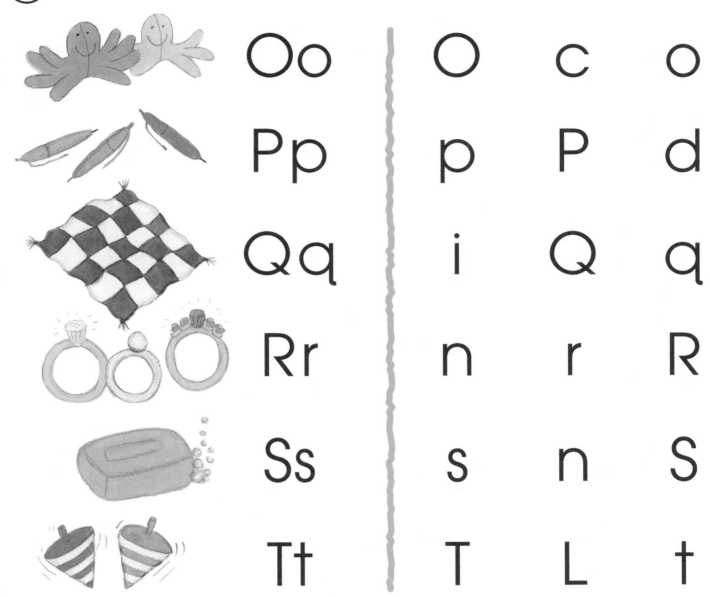

Oo	O	c	o
Pp	p	P	d
Qq	i	Q	q
Rr	n	r	R
Ss	s	n	S
Tt	T	L	t

What is yellow and writes?
A ball point banana!

—Try it! —

Make an alphabet and numeral quilt. Cut out 36 pieces of paper about three inches square. On each one, write a letter of the alphabet or a number from one to ten. Glue the squares in order on a large sheet of newspaper in six rows of six squares.

Language Arts: Alphabet and Beginning Sounds

Shopping for rhymes

The kids bought things with names that rhyme.
Can you find which ones they are?
In each row, color the pictures whose names rhyme.

—Try it! —

It's fun to say silly rhymes with color words.
Start with these and then think up others:
  Yellow, yellow, kiss a fellow;
  Green, green, see the queen.

Where is Lilly?

Oh, dear! Lilly is lost. Help her find Ms. Liz.
Draw a —— along the path she must take.

—Try it!—

What would you do if you got lost in a store?
Talk with your family about it. Make a plan so
you'll all know what to do in case that happens.

Basic Skills: Eye-Hand Coordination   37

Time for a treat

Find crayons that match the colors of the dots.
Color the shapes to discover what the treat is.

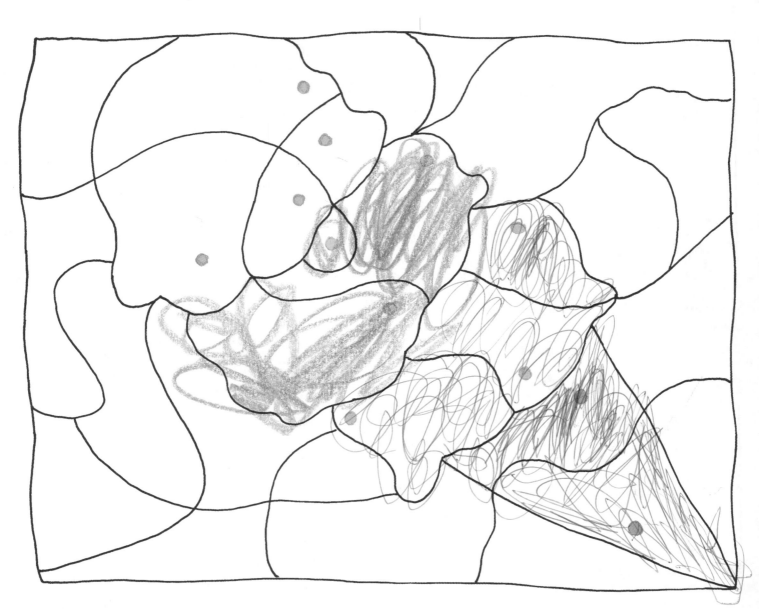

—Try it! —

Ask an adult to help you make a cold dessert. Mix one 14-ounce can of sweetened condensed milk, 2/3 cup chocolate syrup, and two cups heavy cream, whipped. Stir the ingredients together and pour them into a foil-lined loaf pan. Freeze for six hours. Remove from pan. Peel off the foil, slice, and enjoy!

We like ice cream!

◯ the number of servings in each row.
Color the ice cream.

1 2 3 4 5

1 2 3 4 5

1 2 3 4 5

1 2 3 4 5

You scream,
I scream,
We all scream,
For ice cream!

—Try it!—

What's your favorite ice
cream treat? Draw it.

Look at the games!

What are the kids doing?
Use words that tell where.

1. How many s are **high**? _____

2. How many s are **low**? _____

Try it!

It's easy to make sentences. Start by saying a name such as **Lilly**.
Then say an action word: **jumps**. Put the two words together
and you have a sentence: **Lilly jumps**. Now make up more sentences.
Remember, every sentence has a naming word and an action word.

3. How many s are **inside** the tent? _____

4. How many s are **outside** the tent? _____

5. How many s are jumping **over**? _____

Missing numbers

Write each missing number.

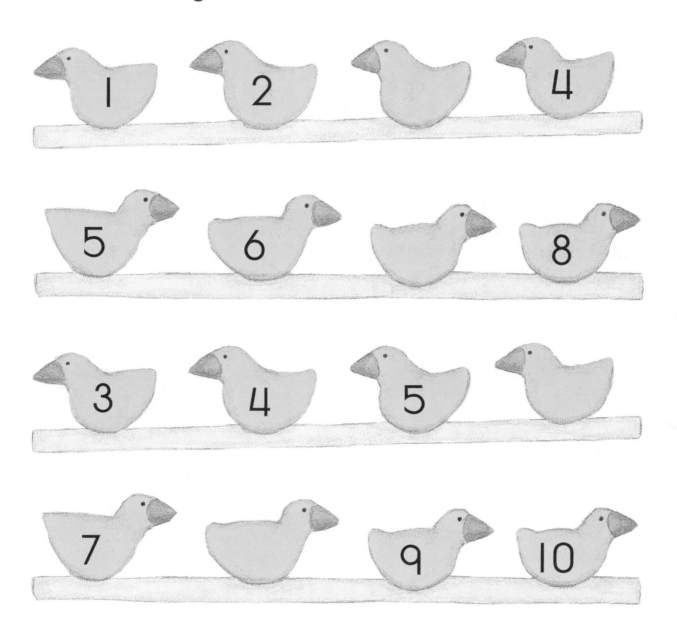

1   2   ___   4

5   6   ___   8

3   4   5   ___

7   ___   9   10

—Try it! —

To do this, you'll need a marker and ten sheets of paper. Trace around your foot on each sheet. Write a number from one to ten on each foot. Then lay out the sheets in order. Can you walk ten "feet"?

That's Wags doing an imitation of a duck!
Get it? He's ducking!

Lots of prizes

What letter begins each picture name?
◯ the capital and lowercase letters.

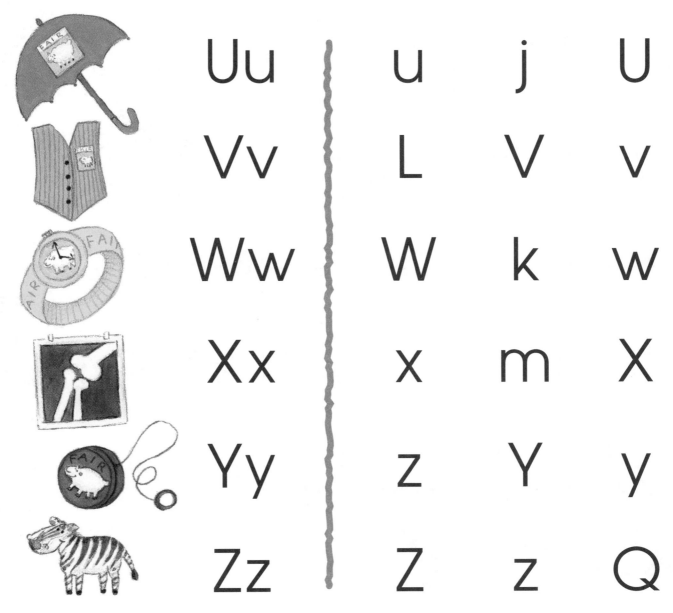

Uu	u	j	U
Vv	L	V	v
Ww	W	k	w
Xx	x	m	X
Yy	z	Y	y
Zz	Z	z	Q

—Try it!—

Make up an alphabet game. Write the letters of the alphabet on a
sheet of paper for an indoor game or with chalk on the sidewalk for
an outdoor game. Throw a button at the letters. Name the letter on
which it lands. Then think of a word that begins with that letter.

Language Arts: Alphabet and Beginning Sounds

Your favorite

What is the most popular ride at the fair?
Color one box for each person on a ride.

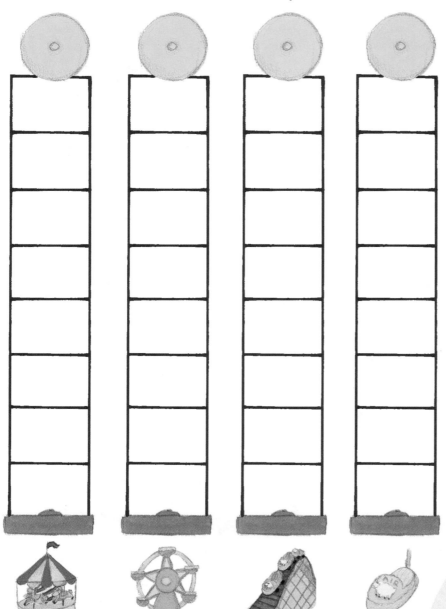

The most popular ride at the
fair is the _____.

─Try it! ─

Ask your family and friends what ride
they like best. Make a graph to show
the rides people like.

What is it?

Follow the dots from **A** to **Z** and you'll find out.

—Try it!—

You may not be able to juggle, but with some practice you can bounce
a ball and catch it. Here's a rhyme to say as you bounce:

    ABCs and vegetable goop.

    What will I find in the alphabet soup?

    A, B, C, D, E . . .

Name a funny word that starts with the letter on which you miss.

This game is fun to play with a friend.

Just-alike clowns

In each row, two clowns are the same.

One is a bit different.

◯ the clown that is different.

-Try it! -

Look at the dishes in your kitchen cabinets. Do you see some that are exactly alike? Are some just a little different? How are they different? Then check the food cupboard. Which cans or boxes are alike?

Basic Skills: Visual Discrimination   **47**

Half a clown

Half of this clown is missing!
Draw her other half.
Then color the picture.

Draw a picture of yourself! (You may want to look in a mirror first.) Notice the color of your hair, eyes, and skin. What are you wearing? You'll want to include your clothes in your drawing, too.

Clowns in a row

Let's measure each clown. Use a .
How many s tall is each one?

1._____   2._____   3._____   4._____

—Try it!—

Measure some of your toys. How many pennies long are
your toy cars? How high is this book? What else can you
use to measure? You might try using your feet, a block, or
even your whole body to measure something big like a rug.

Math: Measurement **49**

Hooray! The sun! ━━━━━

There's a rainbow in the sky.
Read these color words.
Color the rainbow.

red   orange   yellow   green   blue   indigo   violet

─Try it! ─

Get out your watercolors, a paintbrush, and a sheet of white paper.
Experiment with blending colors. Mix red and yellow to get orange
and red and blue to make purple. Mix blue and yellow and what do
you get? Paint a pretty picture with your colors.

Everybody looks!

Color the flowers to finish the patterns.

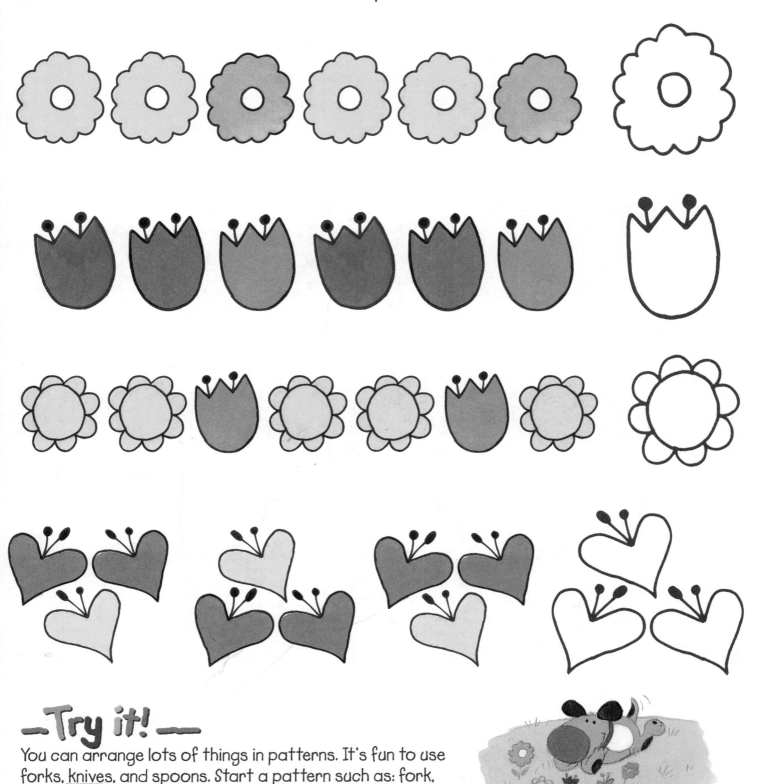

Try it!

You can arrange lots of things in patterns. It's fun to use forks, knives, and spoons. Start a pattern such as: fork, fork, spoon, knife; fork, fork, spoon, knife. Then ask a friend to continue the pattern.

Math: Patterns 51

Smell with your nose

The children are using their five senses.
They are seeing, hearing, smelling, tasting, and touching.
Draw ——s to the sign. Show the sense each is using.

—Try it!—

Tell someone everything Sam can do. Use this sentence
pattern: Sam can _____ with his _____. You might
say, for example, Sam can feel raindrops with his hand.

Time to go home

Do you remember all the things we did today?
Write 1, 2, 3, and 4 to show the order.

—Try it! —

Make a practice clock. You'll need a paper plate, two thin strips of heavy paper for the hands, and a brad to hold the hands in the center. Write the numbers from 1 to 12 around the clock. Then move the hands to make the clock show the same times as the clocks on this page.

We'll remember

Lots of things we saw are hidden in this picture.

—Try it!—

Name seven more things you remember from the fair.
It's OK to look through the book again for help.

○ these in the picture.

Basic Skills: Visual Discrimination **55**

My favorite

What did you like best about the fair?
Draw a picture of it here.
Then tell someone about your picture.

Which joke was your favorite?

Activities to share

Basic Skills

Water Paint Get out paintbrushes and a bucket of water. Children can practice writing letters and numerals on the sidewalk or porch using brushes dipped in the water.

Ketchup Writing Pour a small amount of ketchup into a self-locking plastic bag. Lay the bag on a table and smooth it out to distribute the ketchup evenly. Children can write on the bag with their fingers and then smooth it over to start again.

Play Dough Mix together these ingredients to make dough that will keep for several days if stored in a covered container in a refrigerator.

    2 cups flour
    1 cup salt
    1 cup water
    food coloring (optional)

Cooking with the Senses Cooking engages children's senses of taste, touch, sight, and smell. Cooking also teaches them to measure, plan, observe, and follow directions. Here are a couple of easy recipes for dishes you can make with your child.

Peanut Butter Milkshake

    2 cups milk
    1/3 cup creamy peanut butter
    2 tablespoons honey
    Dash of cinnamon
    4 ice cubes

Measure the first four ingredients into a blender. Blend for 10 seconds. Add ice cubes and blend again. Pour the shake into four glasses.

Saucy Grahams

    For each serving:
    1 graham cracker
    1/4 cup applesauce
    2 tablespoons sweetened whipped topping

Place the graham cracker on a plate. Spread it with applesauce and garnish with a dollop of topping.

Memory Here's a memory game you can play at the supermarket. Before turning into the cereal aisle, ask children to think of three things pictured on the box of their favorite cereal. As you wheel down the aisle, challenge them to find the box. Look at the box together. Did they remember what was on it correctly? Or did they make a wild guess? Play the game again at another time, and they'll be sure to remember every detail.

Activities to share

Math

Shape Sandwiches Cut sliced cheese and bread into circles, squares, rectangles, and triangles for your child to identify. Once that's accomplished, he or she can match the shapes and build them into sandwiches.

Pasta Patterns Necklace String several kinds of hollow pasta, such as ziti, elbow macaroni, and rigatoni on waxed dental floss. Start with a simple pattern and have your child continue it. Children can use watercolors or markers to paint the necklace.

Two-Minute Drills Research suggests that the best way for children to learn math concepts is by manipulating objects, an easy and natural task to accomplish at home. Here are some simple, everyday things your child can do to gain experience using math concepts. You'll think of lots more.

- Estimate the number of peas on the plate; then count them.
- Count the blossoms on a plant.
- Check the temperature.
- Slice an orange in half. How many halves make a whole?
- Count the apples in a bowl. Share one with your child. How many are left?
- Estimate the number of bags you need to hold the leaves you've raked.
- Look at a clock to see if it's time for your favorite show.

If you're in a hurry, make a game of shopping. Engage your child in the race, and see if you can complete the shopping together in a specified time.

Language Arts

Cloud Stories Some sunny day, gather colored paper, white chalk, and a pen. Spread a blanket on the grass, lie on your back with your child, and watch the clouds. What do you see? Elephants? Giant footprints? Flowers? Talk about all the fantastic shapes you see. Your child can then make a chalk drawing of cloud shapes. When he or she is through, write the words your child dictates on the picture. To save the picture, spritz it with hairspray.

Reading Aloud It can't be said often enough: The best way to help your child become a reader is to read, read, read. Set aside a story time each day, perhaps before bed. Encourage your child to turn the pages and "read" aloud to you even if that means memorizing or making up the story. Point to words as you read them. Take delight in the story.

Activities to share

Books You'll Love Here are some books to tempt your kindergartner. They expand on the ideas and concepts presented in this book.

Barn Dance! by Bill Martin Jr. and John Archambault. There's a late-night party in the barn. Be there!

Bootsie Barker Bites by Barbara Bottner. Kids don't always get along!

Country Fair by Elisha Cooper; *Fair* by Ted Lewin. Two handsome books that follow children through their days at a fair.

Science Arts: Discovering Science Through Art Experiences by Mary Ann F. Kohl and Jean Potter. This book includes everything from ice sculptures to magic cabbage to entertain and educate your child.

The Empty Pot by Demi. A Chinese boy plants a seed in this touching fable.

How to Make an Apple Pie and See the World by Marjorie Priceman. Ingredients for an apple pie come from all around the world.

Little Bear Goes to Kindergarten by Jutta Langreuter and Vera Sobat. Little Bear learns that Mama leaves but also returns in this story translated from German.

My Little House ABC, adapted from the Little House books by Laura Ingalls Wilder. An easy-to-read adaptation from the classic series.

A Prairie Alphabet ABC by Yvette Moore. The seasons on a Canadian farm.

Read-Aloud Rhymes for the Very Young selected by Jack Prelutsky. An ever-popular book of lighthearted verse.

The Zebra-Riding Cowboy, A Folk Song from the Old West collected by Angela Shelf Medearis. An educated stranger proves he's not a greenhorn.

Activities to share

Science

Kitchen Science Set out two banana or apple slices. Dribble lemon juice on one. Leave the other plain. After a couple of hours, check the two pieces of fruit. What has happened to them? How has the one without lemon juice changed? Encourage your child to repeat the experiment with other fruits and vegetables. Ask whether all the fruits and vegetables reacted the way the apples and bananas did. How are the fruits and vegetables the same as the bananas or apples? How are they different?

Bug Recyclers After observing fruits and vegetables in the previous activity, put them outside on the ground. Take a look at them every day. Chances are you'll see bugs eating the fruits and vegetables or carrying bits away. They're doing their part to break down and recycle your garbage.

Social Studies

Keep on Trucking Watching trucks can be a lesson in economics. Just think of all the goods and people they carry! See if your child can identify what's in each one. Can he or she find a plumber's truck? An electrician's? A painter's? A landscaper's? Make truck hunting a part of your car trips.

Safety Drill Teaching children what to do in an emergency builds their confidence—and yours, too. Make a fire escape plan and practice it. Be sure your child knows how to dial 911 and give his or her full name, telephone number, and address.

News of the Day From time to time, it's fun to review the events of the day with your child at bedtime. Where did your child go? What did he or she do? Who did he or she see? Expand the discussion to include plans for the next day and recollections of past events. Brief conversations like this help children understand past, present, and future, as well as develop oral language skills.

Answers

Pages 2 & 3

Pages 4 & 5

Page 6

red
blue
yellow
green
orange
purple

Page 7

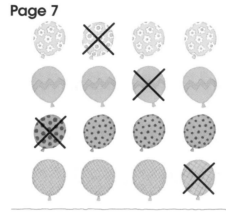

Page 8

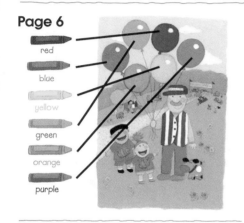

1 ②③ 3   1 2 ③

① 2 3   1 2 ③

Page 9

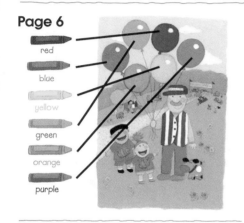

Page 10

Page 11

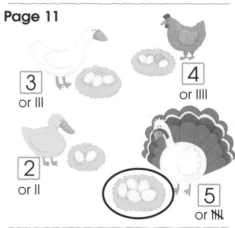

3 or III   4 or IIII

2 or II   5 or ℍℍ

Pages 12 & 13

Children should have drawn mittens.

Page 14

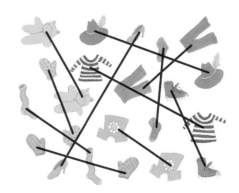

Color patterns in the last row will vary but should be identifiable.

Page 15

Answers

©1999 School Zone Publishing Company

Page 16

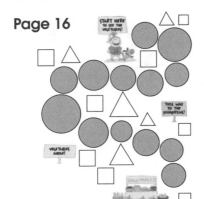

Page 17

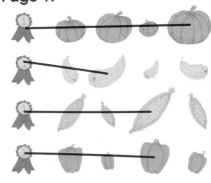

Page 18

Page 19

Children should write their names, addresses, and telephone numbers.

Page 20

   Aa Ⓐ C ⓐ

 Bb ⓑ Ⓑ A

 Cc a ⓒ Ⓒ

Dd Ⓓ ⓓ C

Page 21

How many s? 3 6 2 ④

How many s? ⑦ 4 3 5

How many s? ⑥ 3 5 7

How many s? 4 6 2 ⑤

Page 22

Page 23

 Ee Ⓔ ⓔ C

 Ff d ⓕ Ⓕ

 Gg Ⓖ b ⓖ

 Hh b Ⓗ ⓗ

Pages 24 & 25

    7

   6

   8

   6

Page 26

Favorite rides will vary.

6 kids

Page 27

Answers will vary.

Page 28

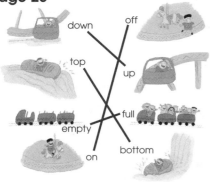

down → off
top
up
full
empty
on
bottom

Page 29

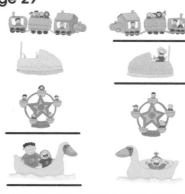

Page 30

Page 31

Drawings should include one food from each of the four groups.

Page 32

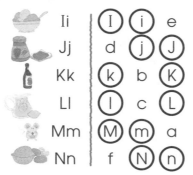

Ii — I, i, e
Jj — d, j, J
Kk — k, b, K
Ll — l, c, L
Mm — M, m, a
Nn — f, N, n

Page 33

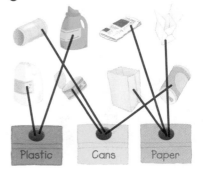

Plastic   Cans   Paper

Page 34

1¢   5¢   10¢   25¢

Page 35

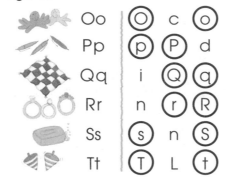

Oo — O, c, o
Pp — p, P, d
Qq — i, Q, q
Rr — n, r, R
Ss — s, n, S
Tt — T, L, t

Page 36

Row 1: Cat, hat, and bat should be colored.

Row 2: Chair, bear, and pear should be colored.

Row 3: Coat, goat, and boat should be colored.

Row 4: Fan, can, and pan should be colored.

Page 37

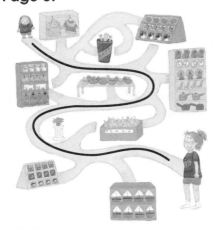

Page 38

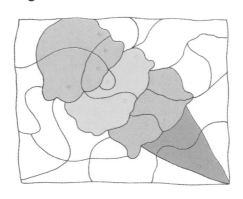

Page 39

1 2 ③ 4 5
1 2 3 ④ 5
1 ② 3 4 5
1 2 3 4 ⑤

Ice cream should be colored in.

Answers

Pages 40 & 41

1. 3
2. 2
3. 4
4. 3
5. 3

Pages 44 & 45

The most popular ride at the fair is the **roller coaster**.

Page 48

Children should draw the other half of the clown and color the picture.

Page 49

1. 7
2. 5
3. 6
4. $4\frac{1}{2}$

Page 52

Page 56

Drawings will vary.

Page 42

Page 43

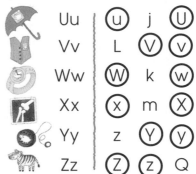

Page 46

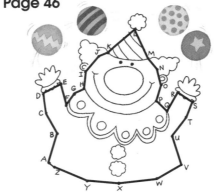

Page 47

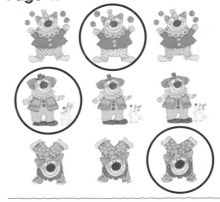

Page 50

Page 51

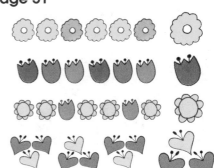

Page 53

Pages 54 & 55

 Kindergarten Scholar 02301